Preparing Children

Information and Ideas for Families Facing Terminal Illness and Death

By Kathy Nussbaum, RN, MS

ISBN 0-9665496-0-0

Cover [top]: Rose with dad, Julio
Rose was five when her dad was diagnosed with brain cancer. During the difficult years that followed and right up through his death, Rose was included in his life and his care in a very special way. [pages: 6, 9, 26 bottom, 29]

Cover [Angel]: Taylor was four when she was diagnosed with a rare form of Lymphoma and died three months later. Although this loss has been profoundly painful, her parents have developed a remarkable way of including their other two children in the grief process. [pages: above, iv top, title page, 11, 20, 34, 36, 44 bottom, 46, 47 top, 54 top; illustrations: iv middle, page 2 and 44 middle]

Cover [middle]: Although Jim's dad had been ill for some time, the news of the terminal nature of his cancer came only days before his death. Jim [age 13] and his siblings have an extraordinarily honest way of expressing their grief. [pages: 15 top and middle, 56 bottom]

Cover [bottom:] Harold's grandchildren learned lessons about living and dying from their grandpa. His willingness to talk about and prepare for his own death will have a lifetime influence on the children who knew him. [pages: 5, 7, 40 top and middle, 49; illustration: page 37 bottom]

Cover and book design:
Cathleen Casey, **Casey Creative** [Eugene, Oregon]

Photography:
Kathy Nussbaum
Adrienne Comadurán   [cover/top, pages 6, 9, 26, 29]
Jeff Fairbanks   [14 bottom, 22 bottom]
Arne Grisham   [pages 28 top, 32, 42 bottom]
Jennifer King   [cover middle, title page, pages 11 bottom, 15 top and middle, 34, 44 bottom, 46 bottom, 47 top, 54, 56 bottom]
Swan Mossberg   [page 30]
Stephanie Randall   [page iv top, 11 top]

Illustrations:
Children's artwork from the Courageous Kids Program: Eugene, Oregon

Table of Contents

Introduction

Your family is traveling down a path which was not chosen and is probably not welcome, yet it remains.

The journey from health to death due to a terminal illness comes without preparation or experience. There are no maps to guide the way, and the inability to see ahead can produce a great deal of anxiety. Fatigue or exhaustion are almost constantly present as the path climbs up with hope and plummets down with disappointment.

Finding the energy along the way to prepare your children for a death and meet their emotional needs may seem a bit overwhelming. Like many parents, you may be unsure about what needs children have during this journey. You may even feel confused as your friends and relatives generously offer conflicting advice about how much to include children during a terminal illness and death.

The following information and ideas were written by Kathy Nussbaum, who has worked in hospice for eight years both as a nurse and as the founder and director of a children's grief support program. She has cared for hundreds of families facing death and bereavement and considers it a privilege to walk with them along this courageous and difficult path of loss, grief and healing.

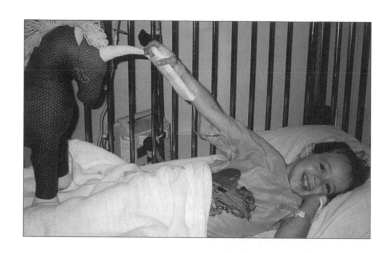

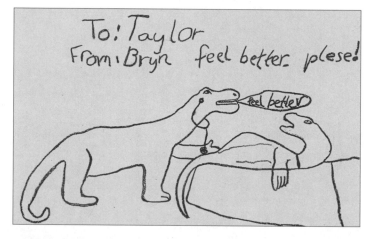

To: Taylor
From: Bryn   feel better. plese!

feel better

[I]

What children need during the terminal illness

The news of a terminal illness will likely feel unreal and hard to grasp at first. You may not even be able to say the word "die," much less discuss death in relation to **your** family. There are suddenly so many things to think about, such mixed emotions, and so much to be done.

What do children need during this time?

Children need information

Although it may seem natural to protect children from painful information related to terminal illness and death, most children cope much better if they are given honest information from the very beginning.

Children over the age of two or three have the ability to figure out that something is wrong when parents get the news of a terminal illness. Adults go to the bedroom to talk, faces look worried or tearful, and there are suddenly many phone calls to or from friends, family or medical personnel.

What children are generally not able to figure out is why all of these things are happening. If they hear bits and pieces of phone conversations, their imaginations may create stories which are inaccurate and highly fearful. They may even think they are somehow responsible for the increased anxiety in the family.

When we avoid giving information to children, it is usually because we are the ones who feel uncomfortable with the subject, not because our children will be unable to cope with it.

Information about the illness

Start by giving children simple explanations. They, like you, may need time to absorb small pieces of information before learning more.

"We just found out that Mom has a sickness that can't get better like most sicknesses. The doctor said it will make her so sick that one day she will probably die."

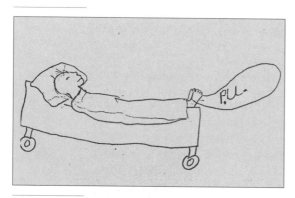

Invite them to ask questions so they can get as much information as they need, but not so much that they get confused. Older children will naturally want and need more detailed information. Sharing it freely will give them permission to talk openly about their own questions and concerns.

Talk about how the terminal illness differs from other illnesses your family has experienced or your children may assume other common illnesses lead to death as well.

Be sure your children know whether or not the illness is communicable and how it is spread. Children often think they can catch cancer or AIDS by simply being close to the person who is sick.

Explain that the illness was not caused by anything they did, said or thought.

Assure them that the doctors and nurses are doing everything they can to make your family member better.

Let them know it is normal to cry or act grumpy when people are sad or worried. Kids often feel frightened by their own reactions, or they worry they are to blame when they see adults crying.

Tell them what you expect to happen in the following weeks and months or the children may think the death could happen at any moment.

Information about death

During this stage of the illness, it may feel that talking about death means giving up hope. However, preparing for a death does not require the loss of hope. A wise patient once said,

> "Prepare To Die - Prefer To Live."

Use the word "die" as you explain death to your children. Other substitute words or phrases may seem easier to say but they can cause unnecessary confusion.

Keep in mind that your children may have some rather distorted ideas about death if they watch television. Talk about the differences between real death and TV deaths.

Ideas

- Look outside and around your house for examples of death. It may be a flower, a bird, or any other form of life which could teach children about the life cycle.

- Ask a friend to go to a library or bookstore to get some books about death. Books provide a wonderful way to approach the subject of death. They also allow time for children to review their content in private. [See Recommended Readings.]

- Keep a record of funny or insightful things your children say or do during this process of death education. When they grow older, they will be curious about how they felt and acted during this time.

3

How children understand death

When giving children information, remember that their understanding of death will be different at different ages. The following age groups are approximate since children vary greatly in their rate of development:

Age 0-2
Infants and toddlers do not have concepts for death or the future, nor are they able to transfer information about a plant or animal death to the death of a person. Giving them information is not as important for them as meeting their physical needs and providing comfort.

Age 2-6
By this age, children are beginning to have a concept of death. They step on bugs and play pretend games with weapons, but their level of understanding about the world still makes it difficult for them to comprehend death.

- **First**, they have confusion about what is alive and what is not alive. To them, cars or toys are sometimes as alive as people.

- **Second**, they have difficulty understanding why things happen. They believe in magical thinking and may think they've caused their loved person's illness by their behavior, actions, thoughts or wishes.

- **Third**, they are not able to grasp the concept that death is permanent. Even if they're told that death will be forever, they may interpret forever as being slightly longer than Mom's or Dad's last business trip.

They are curious about changes they see happening and if they are not given enough information, they will make up explanations which are based on fantasy. It is very important to give children of this age simple but literal information.

Ages 7-11

By this age children can grasp that death is permanent, and they generally understand it is caused by something beyond themselves although there still may be some magical thinking in the younger ones.

They often begin expressing concern and anxiety related to their own death, but they still may not fully understand abstract concepts like heaven.

The body becomes a focus for children of this age. They may be particularly disturbed by physical changes they see happening to their loved person or they may begin looking for changes in their own bodies.

Toono

Teenagers have a full comprehension of death. They understand that death is irreversible and universal, and they can understand the basics of terminal disease processes. They can grasp abstract ideas related to death, and they tend to shut out thoughts of their own death.

Children need to be included

Preparing children to cope with a family crisis involves including them in the changes that are happening and the decisions that are being made.

Changing family routine

Your family routine has probably been altered due to the illness. You may have anything from an occasional medical appointment to a sudden change in your entire schedule. Your children may not know how they fit into this new routine.

Find ways of including them as the routine changes.

Ideas

- Let the children choose a job which they alone are responsible for in the care of the ill person. Possibilities include: reading the paper, giving foot or back massages, serving tea or juice, or decorating the walls with artwork.

- Occasionally allow one child at a time to stay home from school to enjoy the day with the ill person when he/she is feeling particularly good.

- Ask for the children's input regarding new activities your family could do together with strength and energy limitations.

- If possible, choose a doctor who is willing to talk with your children about the illness. Children have a lot of questions but are rarely encouraged to ask them. Asking questions now can prevent years of misinformation.

- Invite the children to join you for an occasional medical appointment so they don't have to imagine what goes on while you are there.

- If your children are shy or intimidated by doctors, encourage them to write down their questions between visits.

- Let them help make decisions about changes that need to be made to the arrangement of the house if medical equipment needs to be accommodated.

Preparations for death

As you make necessary preparations for death, think about ways to include the children. These things require a great deal of energy. Don't wait too long to get started or you may lose the opportunity. Remember, preparing to die does not require the loss of hope or desire to live.

Ideas

- If the ill person is a parent, talk to the children about who will care for them after the death. Children worry about being left without a care provider if something were to happen to the second parent as well.

- Find a funeral home that is good at meeting the needs of children. You may even want to ask if one of the funeral directors would talk with your children or give them a tour of the building. Although this may be difficult for you, your children will likely feel less frightened about going there after the death.

Ideas- for the ill person

- Write a letter to each of your children. Tell them how much you care about them and how much you hate to leave them. Share memories you cherish and explain things you wish had been different between you. You can either deliver the letters personally or ask someone to distribute them after you die. Your children will then be able to read the letters as often as needed for years to come.

- Have your picture taken with each child doing something you have enjoyed together. Pictures are very precious after the death of someone loved.

- Ask a friend to videotape you doing normal activities with your children. You could read a story, play a game, have a conversation or sing a song. Children frequently have fears of forgetting their loved one's voice and facial expressions after a death.

- Tape record your thoughts related to your illness, your life, your struggles, your joys, and your love.

- Invite your children to help you sort through some of your belongings. Organizing your things will prevent a great deal of frustration for others after your death.

- Think about personal belongings that you could give the children as keepsakes. Memorabilia, especially the things you personally give to them, will be very important to them throughout their lives.

Struggle for meaning

Regardless of the age of your children, they, like you, will struggle to understand the meaning of life, pain, illness and death. Don't be afraid to include them in this struggle.

Be honest if you don't have the answers for your children's questions. Simply tell them that some questions don't have answers.

Keep in mind that when children ask questions, they may really be trying to check out their own thoughts. Ask them what they think about the question before you try to answer it.

Child: "Mom, why is Daddy sick?"
Mom: "Why do you think Daddy's sick?"
Child: "Because he caught a bug... I'm never going bug catching again.

You may learn valuable insights about the thoughts of your children by asking them to answer their own questions.

One way to get insight about the meaning of one's life is to invite others to share their perspectives with you and your family.

Ideas

- Have a Celebration of Life party during a time when your ill family member is feeling up to it. Invite friends from all areas of your life and provide a time for sharing comments about ways in which others have been touched by his/her life..

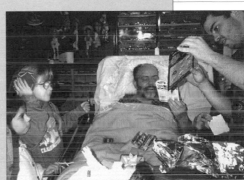

- Compile a book of pages contributed by friends and family and present it to your loved one as a gift. The pages could be entitled:

    Thank you for . . .

    Your life has been a gift to me in the following ways...

    My favorite memories of you include...

    One thing I'll always remember about you is...

    I want to tell you that...

Religious beliefs

If you are a religious family, your faith will likely bring comfort and hope to you as well as your children. Even if you are not a religious family, you will probably find that your children have questions and beliefs related to the afterlife and the meaning of death.

Ideas

- Offer your children a visit to a respected religious leader or friend to discuss their spiritual questions. If you need suggestions about which spiritual leaders in your community are comfortable talking about death issues, ask your local hospice or hospital chaplain.

  - If your religious beliefs include the separation of the spirit from the body, it can be described to children by using a glove and your hand. Put your hand in the glove and explain that as long as your hand [the spirit] is in the glove [the body], it is able to function properly. When your hand is pulled out, the glove looks the same, but it can no longer function.

  - Be sure you clearly explain the finality of death before concentrating on afterlife explanations or your children may become confused. "Mommy is going to live with Jesus" could mean to young children that she will return just as she does when she goes to visit Grandma.

- Many spiritual beliefs include miraculous healings. It is my experience that most terminal illnesses lead to death, even with the greatest of faith. Use caution when talking with your children about healing. Time is precious during a terminal illness and many important things can go unsaid if discussions revolve exclusively around the hope of healing.

Preparing for visits

If your loved person is in the hospital or does not live in your household, take your children for a visit. Several things to keep in mind:

- Children need to be thoroughly prepared for what they will see. Surprises of medical equipment or changes in appearance can be very frightening. Explain in detail what special equipment is for, why appearance changes are happening and how they are to act.

- Remind them that regardless of how the loved person changes in appearance, he/she is still the same on the inside.

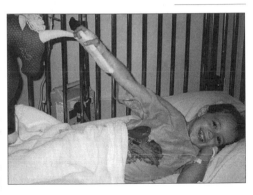

- Encourage the children to take gifts of art, notes, or flowers but not food. Appetites are quite unpredictable during a terminal illness.

- Allow but don't require the children to be affectionate with their loved person. Let them do whatever is comfortable for them.

- Expect young children to make comments that embarrass you such as "Aren't you dead yet?" Don't reprimand them for doing this. They are simply trying to understand what death is about.

- After the visit, talk about how it felt for them. Don't pretend the children didn't notice changes in their loved person.

Children need to express their grief

What is grief?

Grief is the distress we experience when something in our life changes due to a loss. It could be the loss, or anticipated loss of a job, a house, one's dreams about the future, a relationship, or the life of someone loved.

Regardless of the hope for your loved person's recovery at this point, your family has already begun to grieve since news of a terminal illness significantly changes your life.

Every member of your family will experience grief in a different way, with a different set of grief symptoms. The following are some of the more common grief symptoms that children experience during a terminal illness.

Emotional
Anger
Anxiety
Insecurity
Fears [new or increased]
Lack of feelings
Sadness
Depression
Rage
Loneliness
Mood swings
Denial

Behavioral
Trouble in school
Acting "too good"
Regression [bed-wetting,
    thumbsucking, etc.]
Clingy behavior
Aggression
Irritability

Physical
Stomachaches
Headaches
Fatigue
Appetite changes
Sleep disturbances

Psychological
Concentration difficulties
Low self-esteem
Forgetfulness
Confusion
Guilt feelings

Social
Increased conflict with others
Withdrawal

Spiritual
Questions about faith,
    meaning, or the afterlife

It may be difficult to understand how members of your family can grieve so differently from each other. One individual may feel exceptionally anxious or active, wanting to do things, and another may feel constantly fatigued or withdrawn.

Expressing grief

When adults express grief, they generally choose methods that involve the use of words. They may talk about their thoughts or feelings, write about them, or simply think about them, but all of these involve the language of words.

Children, however, are often unable to use words to communicate their inner world. Instead, they speak a language that involves the use of behaviors and various forms of art and play.

These allow them to use symbols rather than words. This language is often so unfamiliar to adults, they don't even recognize it as grief expression.

Behaviors

Very young children often express grief by acting clingy or irritable. They seem to request constant attention during a time when adult energy, patience and time is at a minimum.

Older children may exhibit any of the following behavioral patterns when expressing grief:
Acting out
Withdrawal
"Overly Grown Up" Behavior

Acting out

Children who express their grief by acting out are easy to spot and they seem to find endless ways of getting into trouble. They may start fights, talk back to adults, refuse to do homework, or explode at the slightest incident.

- Children who speak this language of grief may be expressing a number of feelings that can't be spoken with words.

- They may act out as a way of feeling powerful during a time when they feel quite helpless.

- They may unconsciously feel the illness is their fault, and making people angry with them is a way of punishing themselves.

- They may act out around the ill family member as a way of keeping distance from the painful thought of separation.

- They may simply be creating chaos to describe the chaos they feel inside.

13

Anger

Perhaps the most common reason kids act out is that they are just plain angry that the terminal illness has disrupted their lives in such a big way.

Anger is normal during a terminal illness and should not be considered wrong or bad. It is the emotion we experience when we feel we have been violated in some way, and a terminal illness certainly violates life as we anticipate it.

Anger is also the emotion we express when we try to hide a variety of other uncomfortable feelings such as guilt, fear or sadness, all of which are normal during this time as well.

Anger itself is not destructive. It is the way we choose to ventilate anger that determines how negative the outcome will be.

If we give our children the message that it is bad to be angry or show anger, they will learn to direct their anger inward which will set them up for :
Depression
Feelings of guilt or
Physical illness

Our job as adults is to model and teach children appropriate ways of expressing anger that are not hurtful to themselves or others.

Ideas

• Acknowledge how difficult this time must be for them.

• Since children who act out often have extra energy, provide them with activities that involve a lot of physical movement.

- Give the children as many choices as possible in various areas of their lives to help give them a sense of control.

- If you suspect your child may be feeling responsible for the illness, review the cause of the illness, emphasizing that nothing they did, said, or thought contributed to the terminal illness.

- Talk together about anger and the many reasons why kids or adults might feel angry during this time.

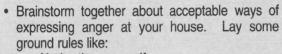

- Talk with your child's teacher or school counselor about ways your child can express anger at school without getting into trouble.

- Brainstorm together about acceptable ways of expressing anger at your house. Lay some ground rules like:
    - No hurting yourself
    - No hurting others
    - No hurting anyone's belongings

- Then let the kids come up with a list of activities they could do when they feel like exploding.

- Don't hesitate to make your own list of ways to express your anger.

- Anger activities may include:
    - Punching pillows, mattresses, or punching bags
    - Beating on molded clay or playdough
    - Screaming in the car
    - Writing or drawing about their anger.
    - Throwing ice cubes at trees or fences
    - Having marshmallow fights
    - Doing strenuous exercises

Withdrawal

Withdrawal is another behavioral language children speak when expressing grief. Children fluent in this language may act as if nothing has changed. They don't act out and they generally don't give much of an indication about how they are doing. In reality, they may actually feel so numb or scared they don't even have words to tell you about how they feel. They tend to get forgotten because they demand so little attention.

Ideas

- Make an effort to spend time with these children, even if they don't ask for your attention. Go for a walk, shoot some baskets or take a drive so you can be physically close together.

- Don't badger them to talk to you about how they are doing. They may not know how they are doing, or their defenses may be temporarily protecting them from information too painful to absorb. Simply be with them.

- If you know you cannot be available to spend private time with these children for whatever reason, ask a trusted friend to help you.

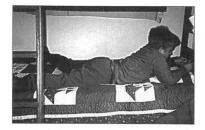

Overly grown-up behavior

Children who act "overly grown up" are often quite pleasant to be around. They are helpful, they try to please others, and they excel in school or extra-curricular activities. Most parents are quite proud to tell their friends how well their child is handling the family stress.

Children may act "overly grown up" in an effort to:
- Relieve guilt.
- Bargain for more time with the loved person.
- "Fix" the family which seems to be falling apart.
- Protect the family from additional stress.
- Avoid facing the pain of reality.

In the long run, the health of these children is at risk. They may develop physical breakdowns when they can no longer maintain their high standards. Eating changes or sleeping disturbances are often the first signs of depression in these kids.

Ideas

- Give positive feedback for the expression of negative feelings.

- Don't expect too much from them around the house, even if they appear to be competent at everything they do.

- Encourage them to spend time with their friends, doing activities that were enjoyable for them before the illness.

- Intervene if you hear friends or family encouraging your children to "be strong" or admiring them for doing so well.

- Assure your children that although they may see you cry or display emotions they haven't seen from you before, they need not feel responsible to take care of you or be strong for you.

17

Art and play

The most natural language children use to process their thoughts and emotions is the language of art and play. Instead of expecting children to talk about their feelings, they should rather be given the opportunity to play out or draw out difficult or painful emotions. Play allows children the opportunity to bring out feelings at their own pace and in their own safe way.

Using art and play, children will tell their own stories using materials that symbolize how they feel. They will take on different roles in an effort to understand their world. In one game they may play helpless victims, and in the next, heroes who conquer evil. Both games can be a child's way of exploring the helplessness he/she may feel.

When children are working through issues about death, they will likely use symbols which represent fear or death in their play.

- They may draw pictures of things that scare them.

- They may include a dead or dying character in their imaginary games.

- They may draw disturbing pictures of fires, dismembered bodies, ghosts or skeletons.

- If the terminally ill person is a parent, they may start including orphans in their play games.

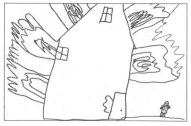

Regardless of what symbols children use, it is frequently disturbing for adults to watch their children play or draw about fear or death. It is a natural tendency to want to tell kids to rather play something "nice." However, this kind of play is normal and healthy and should be encouraged without criticism. The more children can express themselves through symbols, the less control the feelings and fears will have over them.

Although adolescents will probably not use play to express their complex world, they may use various forms of art to disclose their experience. In this way they can express themselves without the terrifying pressure of verbalizing their feelings.

Ideas

• Provide plenty of time to play or draw. Although watching TV for long periods of time may provide you with some needed quiet time, it does not allow time for children to process their feelings.

• Provide various materials needed for art projects or play. If friends ask what they can do for you, suggest they give your children some of the following materials: Art pads, markers, crayons, colored pencils, paints, play dough, clay [some kinds can be baked], puppets, or toys which include people such as a dollhouse, Legos, or Playmobils.

• Encourage your children to keep an art journal if they enjoy drawing. Suggest putting the date and something about the picture they draw or paint on each page.

• If they have trouble getting started, suggest several themes and let them choose one which has meaning for them.
    Draw a picture of Dad.
    Draw a picture of you and Dad together.
    Paint a picture of something that makes you
        sad or mad.
    Mold something out of clay that looks like
        Dad's sickness.
    Draw a picture of somebody who is scared.
    Paint a picture of something you wish you
        and Dad could do together.

Although you will learn a lot from their art or games, avoid interpreting to the children what you see. You may think you see an angel in the sky which is protecting the house below, when in actuality it might be a death ghost which has come to take the entire family. If you say, "What a nice angel," the child may become confused.

If you want to learn more about their games or artwork, simply listen or ask, "Would you like to tell me about your picture?" This gives the child the option of saying "no," and it leaves all of the interpretation up to the child.

Over time you may notice recurring themes in your children's play or art. This may give you a glimpse of the things they are struggling with or the areas in which they need more education from you.

Children Need to Feel Safe

Children generally feel safe when their life is ordered and predictable and when they are surrounded by nurturing friends and family. During a terminal illness, however, a child's world can suddenly become very insecure as they wonder what will come next and who will take care of them.

Although we can't fix a child's insecurity with simple solutions, there are things we can do to increase the feeling of safety for grieving children.

Infants and toddlers

Although infants and toddlers are not old enough to understand terminal illness and death, they are certainly old enough to be affected by them. Disruptions in their normal routine or relationship patterns can be quite disturbing.

They may tell you this with changes in their eating or sleeping habits, or by acting extra fussy or clingy. In addition, toddlers often have regressive behaviors, meaning they are suddenly unable to do things they previously mastered. They may start wetting their pants or insisting on drinking from a bottle instead of a cup. These are all likely indications that they are feeling insecure about their world. What they need most during this time of uncertainty is comfort and routine.

Ideas

* Offer infants or toddlers extra physical contact. Don't be worried about spoiling them.

* Carry an infant around in a pack or play games with a toddler that involve extra physical touch.

* Talk or sing to infants and toddlers in a soothing voice.

* Play calming music in the house.

* Maintain the children's daily routine as much as possible.

* Keep the implementation of new ideas to a minimum. If the terminal illness is unstable, it would not be a good idea to try potty training or weaning a young child.

* Accept your children's need to regress. It is their way of returning to an age of safety. It will be temporary, and scolding will not make it go away.

* If your schedule is so busy or stressful that you simply can't give extra attention to your infant or toddler, ask a friend or relative to help. However, try to avoid getting help from someone your child does not know. Putting an infant or toddler into a new childcare situation could create additional insecurities.

Support

Your children need support both from you and from others throughout this difficult time. Keep in mind that adults in a child's life are not automatically support-givers, even if they are family.

• A support person for a child is someone who has the gift of acceptance.

• Rather than having preconceived ideas about how a child "should" feel or act in this situation, the support person tries to understand the child's perspective.

• Rather than asking the child to express him/herself in the language of adults, the support person accepts the language of the child, even if it is difficult to understand.

• A support person does not keep asking the child how he or she is doing but rather waits for the child to lead the way while simply being available.

Family

Parents are generally their children's primary support system. However, during a terminal illness, it is common for parents to be experiencing so much stress or personal grief that they are unable to be available to their children as usual.

It is also common for children to try to protect their parents from any more pain or tears by keeping their thoughts, questions and fears to themselves.

Ideas

- Get support for yourself! Your children will feel safer knowing they are not responsible to meet your emotional needs.

- Help your children identify adults in their lives who are supportive and encourage them to spend time with these individuals.

- Don't feel you need to do this all alone!

Keep in mind that parents may not be the primary support system for adolescents. Teens often feel their friends are their most valued support givers.

School

School personnel need to be aware of what is happening in your child's life since the terminal illness will undoubtedly affect your child's concentration levels, academic performance and relationships with classmates.

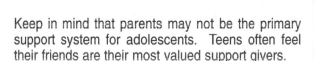

However, be sure to include the child's input as to if, how and when other students should be told about the illness. Well-meaning teachers who announce to the class that a particular student has a dying family member will likely horrify the child rather than provide necessary support.

Most children do not want to be singled out or stigmatized in any way with their peers, regardless of the situation at home.

Friends

Although children instinctively use their friends as a support system, it is common for them to avoid the subject of a terminally ill family member. They may feel embarrassed to bring friends home or ashamed their family is suddenly different than other families. If their feelings of discomfort get too great, they may withdraw from their friends.

24

Attention

Children of all ages need extra attention during this time. They need to know that the ill family member is not the only person in the family worthy of the family's time and energy.

Ideas

• Make a date with each child to do something you both enjoy. Go for a walk, a bike ride or a drive in the car to simply be together. Don't ignore the subject of the terminal illness but don't use this time to get information from them about how they are doing.

• If the children start getting lost in a stream of visitors who come to your house to show support, limit the number of guests. If this is too difficult for you, ask a trusted friend or family member to be in charge of your visitor schedule.

• Lie down close to the children at bedtime. When it's quiet and the lights are out, they may feel safe enough to share their thoughts and concerns with you.

Normal schedule

Although adults often have a completely new schedule when caring for a terminally ill family member, children should not be expected to do this. Rather, they should be encouraged to continue many of the activities which are normal for them.

Ideas

- Don't pull the children out of extracurricular activities. Ask a friend to help with transportation if it's a problem for you.

- Try to have regular meals that include nutritious foods. The kids will be hungry even if you aren't, and it's very easy to let them snack on junk food when your routine is interrupted.

- Don't expect children to sit at the bedside of the ill family member for long periods of time. Let them go out with their friends and play.

- Keep a regular bedtime for the kids that isn't too late. They need plenty of sleep during this time.

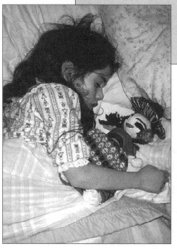

Setting limits

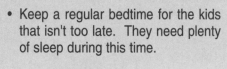

When families are experiencing a crisis such as a terminal illness, it is common both for limit setting to decrease and for children to have increased behavior problems. Parents may not have the energy to discipline as usual, or they may feel that children should be given some slack about the rules due to the situation.

However, even though it may seem unreasonable to be strict about discipline during this time, children actually get a sense of security when they have limits which are consistent and predictable.

If you are having difficulty setting limits for your children, make a new plan that requires less of your energy.

Keep in mind that in order for a limit setting plan to work, rules must be clear, and consequences should be small but consistent.

Idea - Limit Setting

1. Discuss the importance of rules at your house and emphasize the most significant ones.

   Examples:
   No hurting others or their belongings.
   Follow directions the first time you're asked.
   Talk with respect [no put downs or talking back].

2. Acknowledge that rule breaks are often due to increased anger, stress or frustration. Discuss ways of letting off steam without breaking rules.

3. Keep a point chart with two kinds of points one for rule breaks and the other for positive behaviors. Each point could represent phone time, extra time before bed, or time doing chores.

When your child acts inappropriately or breaks a rule, calmly ask him/her to mark a rule-break point on the chart. When you see a positive behavior, ask him/her to mark a positive point on the chart.

To avoid arguments, include the rule that if the child complains about getting a rule-break point, he/she automatically gets another one.

- At the end of the day, tally the points to determine whether the child owes you time, breaks even, or gets extra reward time.

- Certain rule breaks may require immediate consequences such as 5-10 minute work chores.

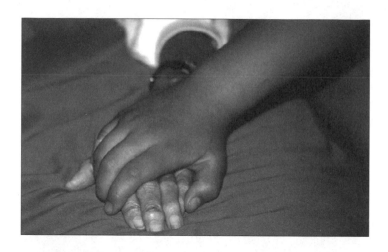

[II]

What children need during the dying process and death rituals

You may be part of a culture that's rich with traditions and rituals around death. On the other hand, if you're like most adults in our country, your experience with death or death rituals is probably very limited.

You undoubtedly wonder what the death will be like and how you will handle the death rituals.

Preparing children for these events involves giving them information about what to expect and including them as much as possible throughout the entire process.

Approaching death

The final stages of life can be a confusing or frightening time for children if they don't have information about why certain things are happening. Not all terminally ill people experience these changes, but the following are things which will require explanation or discussion with your children.

Loss of strength

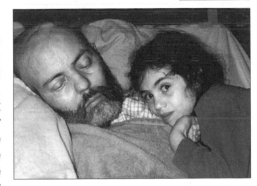

At the end of life, the disease may weaken the body so much that your loved one may need to rest almost continuously. Explain to the children that although the ill family member does not have the strength to talk with them anymore, he/she is still able to hear their voice and feel their touch. You may be able to communicate by using hand squeezes.

Loss of appetite

It is common for terminally ill people to lose their appetite slowly until they may not be able to eat anything at all. Children need to know that their loved person's body can't tolerate normal amounts of food anymore. In some cases eating may simply feed the disease, so the body cuts down on food to protect itself.

Pain or discomfort

Many diseases cause pain or other uncomfortable symptoms. There are many medications these days that can be used to relieve most levels of pain or discomfort. Assure the children the doctors or hospice nurses will do all they can to keep your loved person comfortable.

Personality changes

Some people experience a change in personality as their body weakens. One may normally have a level temperament and suddenly get frequent crying spells or angry outbursts. Your children need to know the disease is influencing these changes.

Confusion

Some diseases cause confusion toward the end of life which can be very frightening for children. If your family member starts saying or doing things that don't make sense, discuss it right away. Don't pretend the children won't notice and don't assume they will understand the person is confused.

Breathing changes

It is common during the last few days or weeks of life for a person's breathing patterns to change. There may be pauses between breaths, the breathing may sound loud and heavy, or it may sound like your loved one needs to clear his/her throat. Explain that these breathing patterns are like snoring - they're uncomfortable to listen to, but the person doing them is unaware of how they sound.

When it's time to make the decision to discontinue treatment for the disease, explain your decision to the children or they may be confused or feel angry that nobody called 911 or tried to prevent their loved person from dying.

The death

Although many adults feel that children should not be present at the death of a loved one, it could be a very positive experience for your children. The transition from life to death is generally more peaceful than anticipated and witnessing this moment first-hand can give children a sense of reality and comfort.

Consider how you, the child's role model, are feeling about being present at the moment of death. If you are feeling frightened or anxious, you may want to consider simply describing the event to them.

If you feel at ease about being present, invite them to join you when you feel the moment of death is approaching. Then leave the decision up to the child. Never force a child to unwillingly be present.

Of course, many people die when their family members are out of the room and the choice of being present is not an option. Because of this, never promise your children they can be present at the moment of death.

It is thought that people close to death somehow know when the time is right to die. Some seem to wait until every last family member has arrived and others seem to wait until everyone has stepped out of the room, as if they want to slip away unnoticed.

Talk with your children about what they imagine the circumstances will be when the death occurs. Assure them they don't need to feel guilty if they aren't present at the moment of death.

When death is close at hand, think about ways of making the transition from life to death as smooth and comfortable as possible. Keep in mind that your loved person will likely be more aware of his/her surroundings than it appears.

Ideas

- Play some favorite music.

- Read a favorite or comforting passage from the Bible or another book.

- Tell stories about memories that come to your mind.

- Touch him/her in comforting ways.

- Give him/her permission to go. It is important for your loved one to know you no longer expect him/her to keep fighting.

- When your loved person finally dies, give yourselves permission to feel relief. It is very normal and does not indicate a lack of love or sadness.

Gone From My Sight

I am standing upon the seashore.
A ship at my side spreads her white sails
    to the morning breeze and
    starts for the blue ocean.
She is an object of beauty and strength.

I stand and watch her until at length
    she hangs like a speck of white cloud
    just where the sea and sky come
    to mingle with each other.

Then someone at my side says,
    "There she goes!"

"Gone where?"

Gone from my sight... that is all.
She is just as large in mast and hull and spar
    as she was when she left my side and
    she is just as able to bear her load of
    living freight to the place of destination.

Her diminished size is in me, not in her.
And just at the moment when someone at my side says,
    "There she goes!"

There are other eyes watching her coming, and
    other voices ready to take up the glad shout,
    "Here she comes!"

And that is dying.

Henry Van Dyke

After the death

Resist the temptation to rush your loved one's body away before the children arrive or wake up. It is usually very helpful for them to see their loved one after he/she has died.

There may be other friends or family who would be grateful for an invitation to join you before you call the mortuary.

When everyone is ready, call the mortuary. When they arrive, you may want to ask them to leave your loved person's face uncovered so you can all say good-bye.

Ideas

- Offer everyone a chance to spend time alone with your loved person. There may be things that need to be said that were too difficult to say while he/she was alive.

- Let the kids climb on the bed or do whatever seems comfortable. They may want to snuggle up to their loved person or they may need to examine the body for missing parts.

- Help children check for signs of death. They may want to listen for a heartbeat or check for breathing.

- Say some prayers. Light some candles.

- You may want to buy a candle large enough to burn continuously from the time of death until the memorial service.

- Give a toast in celebration of your loved one's life.

- Invite friends and family to share memories.

The days between the death and the death rituals

During the days following the death, you will probably be very busy making decisions, talking on the phone, or visiting with guests. Some children love this additional activity and others feel lost with all the extra commotion.

Find time to spend with your children even if you need to leave the house to avoid interruptions.

Ideas

- Explain in detail what the children can expect to happen during these days.

- Decorate a table with flowers, candles and pictures of your loved one. If he/she died at home, you could place the table in the room where the bed was.

- Decide together what clothing or other personal items should be taken to the funeral home to be cremated or placed in the casket.

- Make a secret family list of "Dumb Things People Say After Someone Dies." This gives the children something to do with uncomfortable things they may hear.

- Laugh together about funny things that happen or stories people tell about your loved one. Laughing can be very healing.

- Let the children help answer the phone or record thoughtful things others do for your family.

- Make a plan for what to say if someone calls asking for your loved one. It can be very upsetting if children are caught unprepared.

- Change the message on your answering machine if it includes the name or voice of the person who died.

Death rituals

Children generally have no idea what happens at death rituals. Describing the plans in detail will help ease some anxiety.

Viewing the body

Even if you are planning a cremation, provide children an opportunity to see their loved one's body. Children have imaginative minds and may picture the dead body without a head [because it can't see or hear anymore], or without arms or legs [because in the bathtub we say, "wash your arms, your legs, and your body"].

Seeing the body with their own two eyes will correct their distorted images and help them positively identify their loved one. Children can have dreams for years that the mortuary got the wrong person if they never see their loved person after the death.

Young children may talk in a loud voice in an attempt to awaken their loved person.

They may imagine they see their loved person breathing. It is important to look with them, without criticism, until they are convinced they were mistaken.

Children are naturally curious and may want to touch, poke or push on different areas of the body to see how they feel. This exploration should be encouraged and accepted. Never force a child to touch or kiss the body.

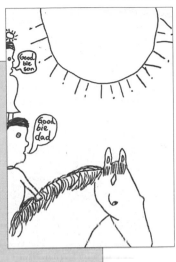

Ideas

- Ask a funeral director to be available to talk to the children if they have any questions related to the funeral home process.

- Put a stool close to the casket so young children can look inside again and again without help.

- Show children the entire body. Some assume the lower half has been cut off since it is covered.

- Provide permanent markers and encourage guests to sign the casket.

- Leave a basket of pencils and index cards in the viewing room and invite guests to write a good-bye note to put in the casket.

- Leave markers and art paper for children who prefer to express their thoughts in a drawing.

The funeral/memorial service

The purpose for a funeral or memorial service is to give friends and relatives a chance to face the reality of death and to reflect on the life of a loved person in an atmosphere of love and support. Children of all ages should be given the opportunity to attend this significant event.

Memorial services can be emotionally painful, but keeping children away does not prevent them from experiencing the pain of grief. It simply gives them the message that they are being excluded from something important. This often results in the feeling of isolation, confusion and resentment.

If the details of the service are explained to children ahead of time, it is likely they will only benefit from observing the ritual and the grief of those who cared for their loved person.

There are many ways to include children in the planning of a service:

Ideas

- They could make a photo display of your loved one.

- They could help pick out items to display which represent the life of your loved one. Things such as handmade items, jewelry, woodworking projects, or favorite pieces of clothing could be included.

- They could help choose photographs or video clips to include in the production of a short video about your loved person.

- They could decorate the church or meeting place with artwork about their loved person.

- Children could make a list of things they love about the person who died and one of them could read it aloud during the service.

- They could read a poem, sing a song, play an instrument, make some comments or pass out programs.

- You could ask a friend or the minister/priest to do a children's story as part of the service.

- Large index cards could be passed out for the guests to write down a favorite memory, a funny story or a word of appreciation about your loved person. The children could then read them again and again as they grow older.

- Have paper and markers available for kids to use during the service. They may not cry or act like they're listening, but they will probably draw about what they're hearing or feeling.

- Videotaping the service would allow young children, or children who chose not to attend the service, to view it later. This is especially helpful for young children who may not remember the service when they get older.

- If your children don't sit with you at the service, make sure they sit with someone who is willing to spend time explaining things to them and answering their questions.

- You could even have a separate service just for kids. It could take place just before the main service and kids could plan it so it would be most meaningful to them. Be sure to leave time for questions.

The burial

We often think of a burial service as the time to release a body back to the earth. However, the opportunity to do this is completely avoided when we neatly hide the hole beneath the casket so it isn't even visible, and then we leave the casket sitting above the ground until everyone is gone. Young children can actually leave the cemetery without understanding that the body of their loved one is going to be buried there.

This confusion can be avoided by simply allowing them to see with their own eyes what will happen to the casket.

Be sure to remind young children that your loved person no longer feels anything so being buried will not hurt him/her in any way.

- Let the children help carry the casket from the hearse to the burial site.

- Show them the hole in which the casket will be placed.

- Allow them to watch the casket being lowered into the ground.

- You could bring shovels and offer the children a chance to help cover the casket with dirt. [Let adults leave if this will be disturbing to them.]

Cremation

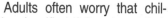

Adults often worry that children will be frightened or horrified if they learn their loved person will be cremated. My experience is that children accept cremation well as long as they are given an explanation as to the reason it was chosen.

Remind young children that cremation will not be painful for your loved person.

Children are usually curious about the cremation process. Young children may want to see or touch the ashes. If they feel comfortable asking questions, they may want to know what the crematorium looks like, what kind of container the body will be in and how hot the fire will get. If you have difficulty answering these questions, ask your funeral director for help.

Following the cremation, include the children in the decision about what to do with the ashes. You have infinite choices about where to distribute them, but don't feel you need to hurry into this. Many families wait for months to come to a decision.

Ideas

- You could have the ashes buried in a cemetery and mark the spot with a special gravemarker. This may be especially important to you if there are other loved ones buried there.

- You may want to plant a new tree or bush in a nearby park and distribute some ashes around its base. This would give you a chance to watch the tree grow and change, as you will, over time.

- You could brainstorm together about your loved person's favorite places or places you enjoyed as a family. These could include anything from a shopping mall to a favorite hiking trail. Then figure out how to discreetly place some ashes in one or more of those places.

This can be a very healing process if you don't rush into it.

Consider putting at least some of the ashes in a place that is close and accessible for those who need a specific place to go to grieve their loss. If you put them in your yard and you move away at some point, you will not have access to that area anymore.

Returning to school

Children will have a variety of responses to the thought of returning to school following the death. Young children may be anxious to get back to school to tell everyone about the death while most older children dread the thought of returning to school.

Friends and school staff are rarely comfortable in knowing how to deal with a bereaved child. Most will either ignore the subject of the death or they will baby the child, both of which are extremely uncomfortable for the returning student.

Ideas

• Talk with your children about how they would like the topic of the death to be handled in their own classrooms and share this information with their teachers.

• Warn the children that most people won't know what to do to comfort them and that hurtful things might unintentionally be said or done.

• Continue your family list of "Stupid Things People Say or Do After Someone Dies." Laughing is a great way to heal from hurtful comments.

• Give the children a small item, like a smooth rock or a personal belonging of your loved one, to put in their pocket. When they start to feel worried, they can reach for the item and rub it to relieve their anxiety.

I DIDN'T GET TO SPEND MUCH TIME WITH HER

[III]

What children need to heal from their loss

Healing from a significant death is a process that spans over an entire lifetime. The pain of the loss, however, decreases over time provided the children have their grieving needs met.

Children need to acknowledge that the loved person has died

Before children can grieve the loss of someone loved, it is necessary for them to confront the reality that someone significant has died and will not be returning.

Even though your children may have known your loved one was going to die, it might still come as a surprise to them, especially if they became accustomed to a lot of ups and downs during the illness. It may take several months for them to acknowledge the death. If the illness was a recent diagnosis or information was distorted or withheld from them along the way, it may take even longer.

If you haven't already done so, provide the children with a meaningful way of saying good-bye to your loved one.

Children Need To Remember

Acknowledging the death does not mean the relationship with the loved person is over. Healing involves the development of a new relationship which is one of memory rather than presence.

Children often get subtle messages that it's best to forget what has happened and move on. This is communicated when adults avoid talking about their own memories. Some households even have an unspoken rule that the loved person is never to be mentioned again.

This may seem like the easiest way to get on with your lives but the long term results can be devastating to the children's physical and mental well-being. The only way for children to find hope and healing is by embracing their memories.

Ideas

- Talk freely about your own memories, even if it brings tears.

- Ask the children about some of their memories.

- Let the children pick out keepsakes from your loved one's belongings. If the children are quite young, save some things to give them when they get older.

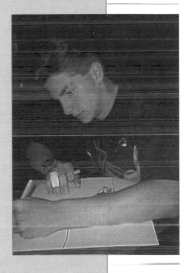

- Get duplicates or enlargements made of your children's favorite photos so they can keep them in their room.

- Make a scrapbook or picture collage of your loved person.

- Get the children an art pad, journal or workbook to record memories.

- Hang a graffiti board in the bathroom entitled "Things I Miss About _____." Let each family member contribute to the board as they wish.

- Read some children's books about remembering loved ones who have died. [See Recommended Readings.]

- Ask friends and relatives to talk about their memories

- Visit places of special significance.

47

- Find a special place to plant a tree or some bulbs in memory of your loved person.

- Tell each other about or draw the dreams you have of your loved person, even if they don't make sense.

In addition to good memories, your children probably also have some unpleasant memories of the person who died. These memories will also need to be embraced and shared in order for healing to take place.

Assure your children that it's normal to remember unpleasant things after someone dies and give them permission to share those memories with you or another support person.

If memories include those of physical, sexual or emotional abuse, professional help will be needed before your children will be able to mourn their loss.

Holidays and other special days

Bereaved families experience a great deal of distress around the holidays, the anniversary of the loved person's death and other significant days of the year.
Some families valiantly attempt to celebrate these special days

as if the loss never happened. Although tension is high and there is an obvious hole without the loved one, the subject of the loved one is never mentioned. This rule of silence is quickly learned by the children and usually results in many years of strained family gatherings.

Others families cancel holidays or special days completely, resulting in great loneliness as each family member is left alone in their grief. Children are particularly disturbed by the loss of family traditions in addition to their loved one.

Holiday or special day rituals can offer healing if you are willing to face your pain. Start by openly acknowledging that this year's holidays and other significant days will be difficult. Make a family plan to prepare for them. Talk about which traditions you want to continue and which you would like to change.

Build into your plans specific ways of honoring the memories of your loved person on special days. The children need to know that the significance of their loved one did not end with his/her death.

Ideas

- Look at photo albums or home videos from years past.

- Visit the gravesite to plant bulbs or have a picnic.

- Take a trip you wish you could have taken together.

- Take flowers to a place your loved one worked or volunteered.

- Give a gift to an organization your loved person cared about.

- Request your loved one's favorite song on the radio.

- Have a gathering of friends who helped your family through the illness and death.

- Pass out art materials and invite everyone to draw a picture of their favorite holiday memories.

- Let each member of your family make a collage of their favorite holiday photographs.

- Return to a previous vacation spot.

- Have your loved one's jewelry altered or made into new pieces for you or your children.

- Buy a special memorial candle to light on each significant day.

- Declare the anniversary of the death a family holiday and spend the day doing things your loved person enjoyed.

- Have a potluck and ask each guest to bring a dish that your loved one enjoyed eating.

- Plant a memorial flower garden.

- If it was a mom who died, keep in mind that young children make projects in school for Mother's Day. Plan ahead for what your children will do during this difficult time.

- Treat yourselves to a box of extra soft tissues for the tears that will naturally flow on these significant days.

Children need to feel and express the pain of loss

> "Time does not heal a painful loss...
> Grieving does."
>
> Anonymous

We often want to believe that time alone will provide healing following a significant death. We quickly move the children away from uncomfortable feelings, and we keep ourselves busy to avoid facing the pain of loss. However, it is moving toward the pain that ultimately heals.

Children express pain differently at various ages and at different stages of the grieving process. Their reactions also depend on who died, how long the individual had been sick, and how prepared they were for the death.

The following are some generalizations about how children of various ages react to death and express the pain of loss. Please keep in mind that what works with one child may not work with another.

Age 0-2

Toddlers often initially express feelings of loss by looking repeatedly for the person who died. They may look in a familiar spot or in the place the loved one was last seen.

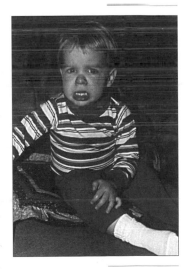

If they are able to talk, they may ask for the person over and over. They may scream or act angry to try to bring their loved person back.

Eventually the toddler will give up hoping for the loved one's return and sadness will set in. The child may become temporarily uninterested in food, toys or activities.

Regressive behaviors may be noted. The child may temporarily stop talking or go back to crawling.

A child of this young age could have lasting vulnerabilities to separation and loss if support is not given.

Ideas

- Provide physical comfort. It may not immediately ease the pain of separation, but it will eventually facilitate healing.

- Accept the child's regression without criticism.

- Give the child a piece of clothing that still has the loved person's smell on it.

- Give the child a picture of their loved person to carry around.

- Make up a photo album from extra pictures of your loved one and keep it in a place that is accessible to the child.

Age 2-6

Parents often perceive children at this age as being relatively unaffected by the death. They may go outside to play shortly after hearing the news of the death and they rarely cry at first. They may act as if they aren't grieving at all.

They may do or say things that seem inappropriate to adults.

At some point they start displaying behavior changes such as increased anger, regression or clingy behavior.

They often have new or increased fears and nightmares for some time after the death.

At this age children are not able to understand abstract concepts such as heaven. They may picture it as a bunch of dead bodies laying all over the ground or a place like jail where people are forced to stay against their will.

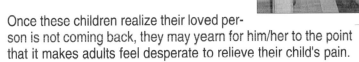

The concept of forever is also too abstract. They may ask if they can write a letter to their loved one to beg him/her to come home, as if he/she could choose to come back.

Since they believe in magical thinking, they may think they have caused the death in some way, even if they observed the entire illness and dying process.

Once these children realize their loved person is not coming back, they may yearn for him/her to the point that it makes adults feel desperate to relieve their child's pain.

Children in this age group move toward pain primarily by using art and play. They may turn the couch into a casket, they may pretend someone has died, or they may draw angels and caskets or other death symbols. This is very healthy and should be encouraged.

Ideas

- If your family talks about heaven, encourage your children to draw pictures of what it must look like so you can get a glimpse of the images they have in their minds.

- Give positive comments about your child's death play and art and make suggestions for further exploration.

- Be patient as you repeat information about death's permanence.

- Set limits for inappropriate behavior and accept your children's regression.

- Provide comfort when your children have nightmares and encourage them to draw their dreams if they remember them the next morning.

Age 7-11

By this age, children have a much greater understanding of the future and therefore what the loss will mean to them.

Even though they yearn for the person who has died, they often hide their tears because they don't want to appear childish or helpless.

They don't want to be different in any way from their peers, and they are very sensitive to teasing from other children about the death.

Because they're aware that they too could die, these children may become fearful of sleep or darkness, or they may worry that their own aches and pains could lead to death.

They may try to hold on to their loved one by adapting his/her behaviors or mannerisms. Photos and objects which belonged to the person who died are particularly important for children of this age.

They have a well developed capacity for feelings of guilt and they often have regrets about things they did or didn't do before the death, especially if the loved one was a sibling.

Although children in this age group are more capable of language, they tend to express their grief in art, stories, music, play and aggressive behaviors.

There tends to be a lot of aggression problems in school, especially for boys. There may also be regressive, withdrawn or overly grown-up behaviors.

Ideas

- Encourage keeping a journal, drawing pictures, or writing stories, poems or music about their feelings or experiences.

- Allow for energy release through physical activities.

- Set limits for aggression and accept regressive behaviors.

- Model and encourage the expression of a range of emotions.

- Create family rituals that encourage releasing feelings of guilt. Writing letters to the person who died may be helpful.

- Work with the school about academic problems.

- Help educate your children's friends about how to be supportive.

- Offer reading materials to be read alone or together. [See Recommended Readings.]

Teens

Teenagers may feel they need to be strong so they can care for the rest of the family. Their pain tends to express itself through physical symptoms, depression and anger.

They will likely be moody and they may become bossy in an effort to appear powerful and in control.

They frequently express anxiety about the death by being reckless with their own lives to show they are not vulnerable to death. They may drive at high speeds or abuse drugs or alcohol.

Girls may increase sexual activity in an attempt to receive physical comfort. Boys may seek body contact and tension relief by fighting or becoming aggressive.

There are usually problems with dropping grades in school, even if the death was expected for quite some time.

This can be a very confusing time for teens as they struggle to become independent from their parents, yet suddenly find themselves feeling helpless and dependent.

Language is the way teenagers most often express their feelings of grief. They may feel, however, that emotional expression is not acceptable to their friends.

Ideas

- Watch for reckless or impulsive behaviors.

- Set limits but don't become too controlling.

- Be available to them and encourage getting support from others.

- Children of all ages often feel alone in their grief. Consider taking your kids to a children's bereavement support group in your community.

There they will discover they are not alone, they will find that their feelings are normal, and they will learn valuable coping ideas from other children.

- Consider attending a support group of your own. The more comfortable you feel with your own grief, the more you can be of help to your children.

- Offer books about teen grief or purchase a teen grief workbook for their own private use. [See Recommended Readings].

Complicated grief

Most children experience normal grief after the death of someone loved. However, if children have had other losses or difficulties in their lives, they may experience what is called complicated grief, which could require counseling.

Although many of the following symptoms are considered normal, they could become warning signs of complicated grief if they last more than 6 months or so.

- Denial of the death
- Depression
- Aggression toward self or others
- Feelings of guilt about the death.
- Fears or anxiety
- Physical complaints without medical findings
- Changes in sleeping or eating habits
- Drug/alcohol abuse or thoughts about suicide [require immediate help]

If you have questions about whether or not your child may need extra help during the grief process, don't hesitate to ask your school counselor, doctor or local hospice for advice.

Children need to integrate the death into their lives

The death of a family member forever changes a child's understanding of the world. Healing requires that the child find meaning in the death, develop a new self-identity and reinvest his/her emotional energy in other relationships.

Search for meaning

Starting at a young age, children wrestle with "How?" and "Why?" questions in an attempt to understand what purpose the death had in their lives. This search for meaning can take years, and it often results in a wisdom about life that can be gained only when one experiences a great loss.

It is in struggling that children gain wisdom and personal growth, not in hearing simple explanations. Don't make the mistake of feeling you need to provide answers to all of their questions. You will be most helpful if you admit that you, too, are struggling to find meaning in the death of your loved one.

New self-identity

Children often understand themselves in terms of their relationships with other people in their lives. They may think of themselves primarily as a younger brother or "Daddy's little girl." Thus when someone in the family dies, they must reestablish who they are without the loved person.

Many children experience regressive behaviors during their quest to discover their new self-identity. This is a very normal way for children to express their need for support and safety. As your child heals, the need for regressive behaviors will lessen.

After a death, children must also redefine their roles in the family. Jobs that used to be done by the person who died must now be distributed among the remaining family members. Children often describe this as being a very difficult adjustment.

Be careful not to expect too much from your children. They should not be expected to act like grown-ups, and they should not be encouraged to be "the man or woman of the house" under any conditions.

If possible, wait for a while before moving, changing child care situations or selling family possessions. It will be much easier for them to adjust to one change at a time.

Reinvesting emotional energy in others

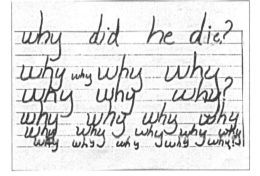

If children experience a great deal of pain with their loss, they may be afraid to love anyone again or they may feel that developing new relationships would be disrespectful to the person who died.

As your children learn to adjust to the death of your loved one, it will be important for them to reinvest their emotional energy in new relationships and learn to love again.

[IV]

Conclusion

Grief varies in length and intensity depending on one's personality, available support, the size of the loss or anticipated loss, and the history of other losses in one's life.

As your children grow and reach new developmental stages, they will regrieve their loss again and again with new levels of understanding. This is quite normal and should not cause concern.

They will need your continued support throughout their lives as they discover new meaning related to the changes they have experienced during the grieving process.

Blessings to you and your family as you continue your courageous journey through grief.

Changes

Just as when the waves
Lash at the shore,

The rocks suffer no damage

But are sculpted
And eroded
Into beautiful shapes,

So our characters can be molded
And our rough edges
Worn smooth

By changes.

Sogyal Rinpoche

[V]

Recommended Reading

Books

Children and young people

1. **Annie and the Old One**. Miles, Miska. Joy Street Books, 1971. Native American grandmother prepares to die. Ages 7-11.

2. **Badger's Parting Gifts**. Varley, Susan. Lothrop, Lee & Shepard Books, 1984. Memories. All ages.

3. **Daddy and Me**. Moutoussamy-Ashe, Jeanne. Alfred A. Knopf, 1993. Daughter of Arthur Ashe talks about her daddy's AIDS. Ages 3-10.

4. **Daddy's Chair**. Haas, Shelly. Kar-Ben Copies, 1991. Father death. Jewish culture. Ages 4-8.

5. **Everett Anderson's Goodbye**. Clifton, Lucille. HenryHolt & Company, 1983. Father death. Ages 4-8.

6. **Gran-Gran's Best Trick**. Holden, Dwight, M.D. Magination Press, 1989. Grandpa's terminal illness and death from cancer. Ages 7-11.

7. **How It Feels When A Parent Dies**. Krementz, Jill. Alfred A. Knopf, 1981. Collection of stories written by kids. Ages 8-18.

8. **I Carried You On Eagle's Wings**. Mayfield, Sue. Lothrop, Lee & Shepard Books, 1990. Mom dies of terminal illness. Ages 12-18.

9. **Learning To Say Good-Bye When A Parent Dies**. LeShan, Eda. Macmillan Publishing, 1975. Ages 7 and up.

10. **Lifetimes: The beautiful way to explain death to children**. Mellonie Bryan & Ingpen, Robert. Bantam Books, 1983. The life and death of plants, animals and people. Ages 3-11.

11. **Losing Uncle Tim**. Jordan, Mary Kate. Whitman Niles, 1989. A boy copes with his uncle's death from AIDS. Ages 5-11.

12. **Mama's Going To Buy You A Mockingbird**. Little, Jean. Puffin Books, 1984. Dad dies of Cancer. Ages 12-18.

13. **Nadia The Willful**. Alexander, Sue. Alfred A. Knopf, 1983. Brother death. Memories. Ages 7-adult.

14. **Old Pig**. Wild, Margaret. Dial Books for Young Readers, 1995. Grandma prepares to die. All ages.

15. **On The Wings Of A Butterfly**. Maple, Marilyn. Parenting Press, 1992. Child with terminal illness. Ages 5-18.

16. **Pablo Remembers**. Ancona, George. Lothrop, Lee & Shepard Books, 1993. Mexican day of the dead fiesta. All ages.

17. **Talking About Death**. Grollman, Earl. Beacon Press, 1990. General information about children's grief. Section for children. Adults & ages 4-8.

18. **Teenagers Face to Face with Bereavement**. Gravelle,K., Haskins, C. Julian Messner, 1989. General grief information. Teens.

19. **The Empty Place**. Temes, Roberta. Small Horizons, 1992. Sister dies of terminal illness. Ages 7-11.

20. **The Two Of Them**. Aliki. Greenwillow Books, 1979. Memories of Grandpa. Ages 4-11.

21. **When Dinosaurs Die**. Brown, Laurie & Marc. Little, Brown & Company, 1996. General book about death and grief. Ages 4-11.

Parents

22. **The Grieving Child**. Fitzgerald, Helen. Fireside, 1992. General information about children's grief. Adults.

23. **How To Help Children Through a Parent's Serious Illness**. McCue, Kathleen. St. Martin's Press, 1994. Information for adults.

24. **Just You and Me**. Richmond, Judy. Hands of Hope Hospice, 1995. Activities and ideas for families during a terminal illness.

Workbooks/Activity books

Children and young people

1. **A Keepsake Book Of Special Memories: Helping Children Heal From Loss**. Van-Si, Laurie. Continuing Education Press. PSU Portland, OR 97207. 1994. Ages 5-11.

2. **Fire In My Heart-Ice In My Veins: A Journal For Teenagers Experiencing A Loss**. Traisman, Enid Samuel. Centering Corporation, 1531 N. Saddle Creek Rd. Omaha, NE 68104. [402] 553-1200. 1992. Teens.

3. **Forever In My Heart**. Levine, Jennifer. Mt. Rainbow Publications, 1992. Parent terminally ill. Ages 7-11.

Preparing the Children

Information and Ideas for
Families Facing Terminal Illness and Death

Order Form

Date: _____

Name: _____

Organization: _____

Address: _____

City/State/Zip:

Phone:

Price per Book
1 0 oopy: $8.05
10+ copies: $4.95

Shipping/Handling
1 book $3.50
2-9 books $5.00
10-24 books   Number of books x $0.65
25+ books   Number of books x $0.45

Cost

_____ Number of copies

_____x_____ Price

_____ Subtotal

_____ Shipping/handling [Maximum $25.00]

_____ **Total**

Write checks and send to:
Gifts of Hope
P.O. Box 8981
Kodiak, AK 99615
[907] 486-6997

Preparing the Children
Information and Ideas for
Families Facing Terminal Illness and Death

For ordering information, please contact:

Gifts of Hope
P.O. Box 8981
Kodiak, AK 99615
[907] 486-6997